I know that sounds **!nsane** but just give me a moment and allow me to explain.

We **do not fly** around in spaceships
and we do not live **in outer space**.

However, one night, he just **showed up**
and **landed here** without a trace.

WELCOME
TO EARTH
BABYBROTHER

When I try to talk to him, he just puts up his hand,

and speaks a language no one can **understand**.

Mommy and daddy swaddle him in his jammies

and say **he is so cute**.

They can´t fool me!

I know it´s a spacesuit!

He opened up his mouth

and I saw what was underneath.

There wasn't **anything** there!

He did not have any teeth!

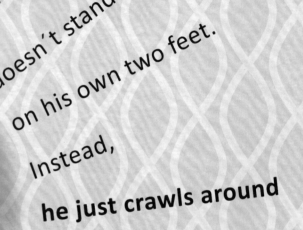

He sometimes
doesn't stand up
on his own two feet.
Instead,
he just crawls around
on his hands and knees.

He can´t eat **solid food**,

only in liquid form.

It can´t be **too hot**,

it can´t be **too cold**,

it has to be **lukewarm**.

His breath can be **so stinky**
from foods from another planet.
When I smell it, I have to run away
because I just can't stand it!

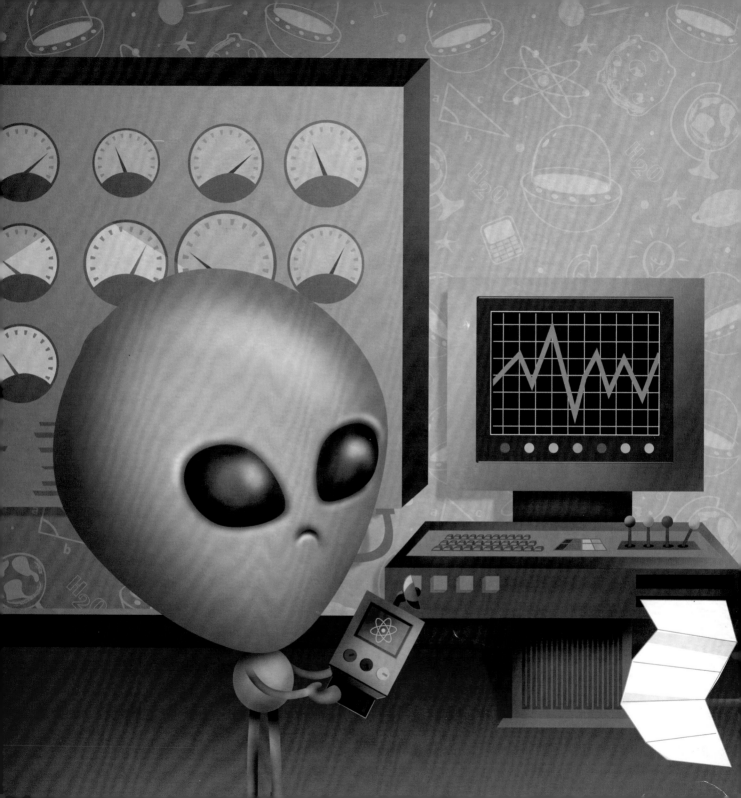

We have a device

that monitors him

at all times,

but I think

he wants to use it

to try to read

our minds!

He keeps me up all night

with his screams and cries.

I think he is contacting

his home planet

so they can send

more alien guys!

At night, **I lock** the door to my bedroom

and I throw away the key.

I might get abducted!

That's what worries me!

I saw his diapers and my eyes became teary, because they were really gross and **very scary!**

The diapers **were bad**,

they really smelled!

I took off running

and I screamed

and yelled!

I can´t believe it!

The evidence is clear.

My brother is **from a planet**

no where **near here**.

I think **my little brother is an alien!**

I must tell mom and dad.

I hope they don´t get upset,

I hope they don´t get mad.

Possible alien brother
loose in your neighborhood.
Protect all toys and candy
and stay indoors
for your own good.

ALIEN
BROTHER
ALERT

Mommy! Daddy!

Look! It's my brother!

I told mommy and daddy about my brother and they laughed out loud! They said, "you have a silly imagination, your brother is not an alien, **he is just a baby.** We love you and you both make mommy and daddy very proud."

ISBN-10:0-615-97642-5

ISBN-13:978-0-615-97642-6